This book is dedicated to *Desmariah, Melodee* and the young girls who dare to dream. No matter the circumstances, you can succeed.

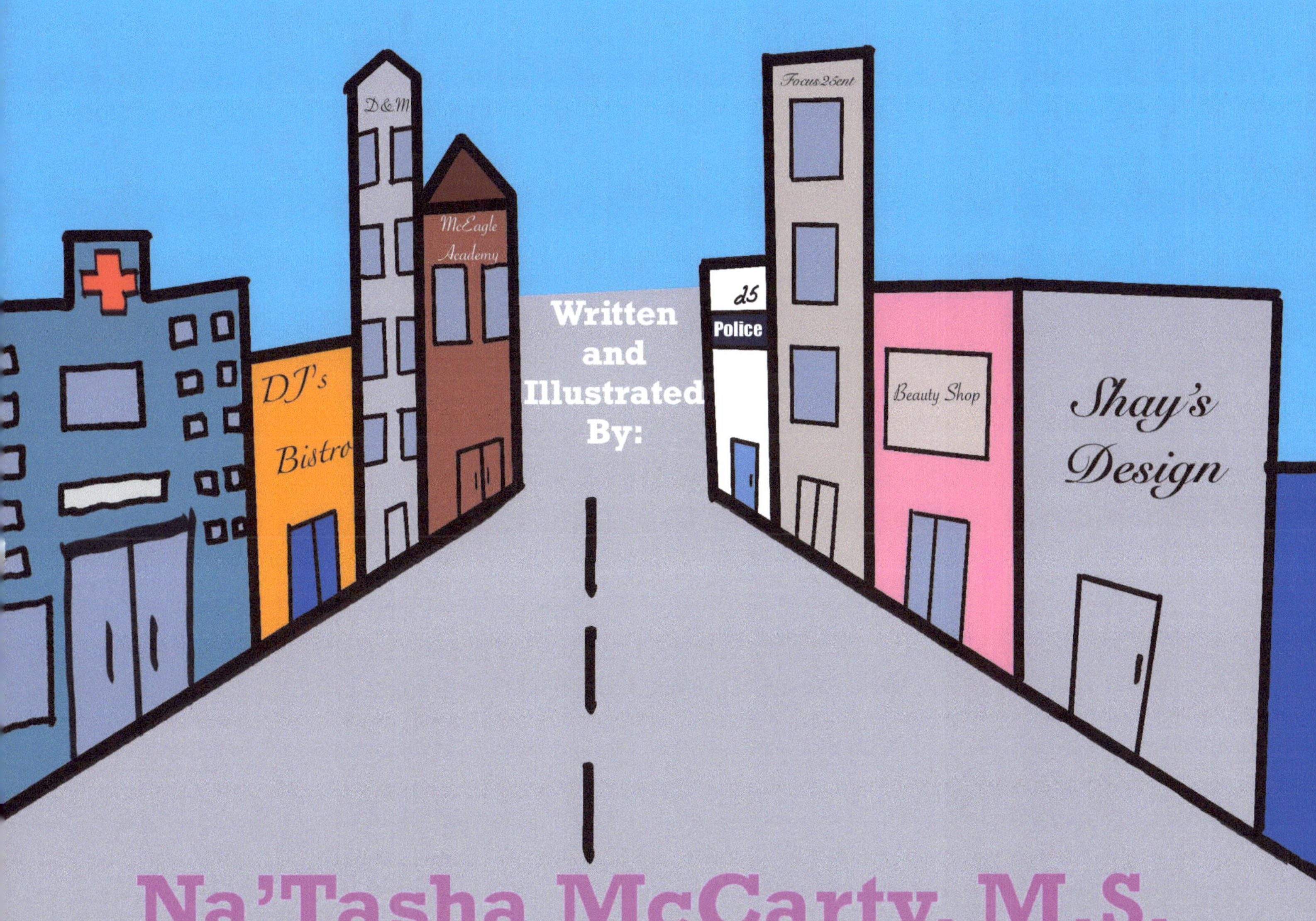

You Can Young Queen

Written and Illustrated By:

Na'Tasha McCarty, M.S.

You Can Young Queen. The world is full of possibilities and with hard work and persistence you can achieve anything. What can you achieve you may ask? Let's see the possibilities!

You can be a *Doctor* or *Surgeon* if you choose. If you like science and helping people this could be for you. These jobs help keep people healthy, help people when they get injured and help people when they are sick. If you stay motivated and work hard, *you can*.

What about an *EMT* or *Paramedic*? These jobs help people when there is an health emergency such as an injury or an accident. They help people feel better and transport them to the hospital. These jobs also serve the community. With persistence and determination, *you can.*

If you like science and helping people, you may want to be a *Pharmacist*. A pharmacist explains and gives people the medicine they need to feel better. If you continue to stay motivated and work hard, *you can.*

You can be a *Police Officer* if you choose. This job helps people stay safe. They also protect and serve the community. With persistence and hard work, *you can*.

You Can Young Queen

What about becoming a *Teacher*? This job helps people explore and learn new things. This job also helps people discover their passions. With persistence and hard work, *you can.*

You can be a *Business Woman* or *CEO* if you choose. These jobs run companies in order to make money and to help many people in the community. If you're a leader, visionary, daring, and determined this may interest you. Well, if you stay motivated and work hard, *you can.*

You Can Young Queen

You may want to be a *Lawyer*. A lawyer works in a court room to advise people on the law. If you like to defend people and fight for justice and equality then this may be for you. If you continue to stay motived and dedicated, *you can*.

Perhaps you might want to go further and become a *Judge*. A Judge listens to evidence that lawyers present in a case and makes rulings on cases. If you believe in fairness and justice this may be for you. With persistence and hard work, *you can.*

You Can Young Queen

Do you like to draw and create? If so, you can be a *Graphic Designer*. This career allows you to use your imagination as well as use technology to create amazing works of art. This job also helps companies bring their business designs to life. Well, if you stay dedicated and work hard, *you can*.

If you like technology and working on computers you might want to be a *Software* or *Computer Programmer*. These jobs create computer programs, applications and games using science and technology. With persistence and determination, *you can*.

You Can Young Queen

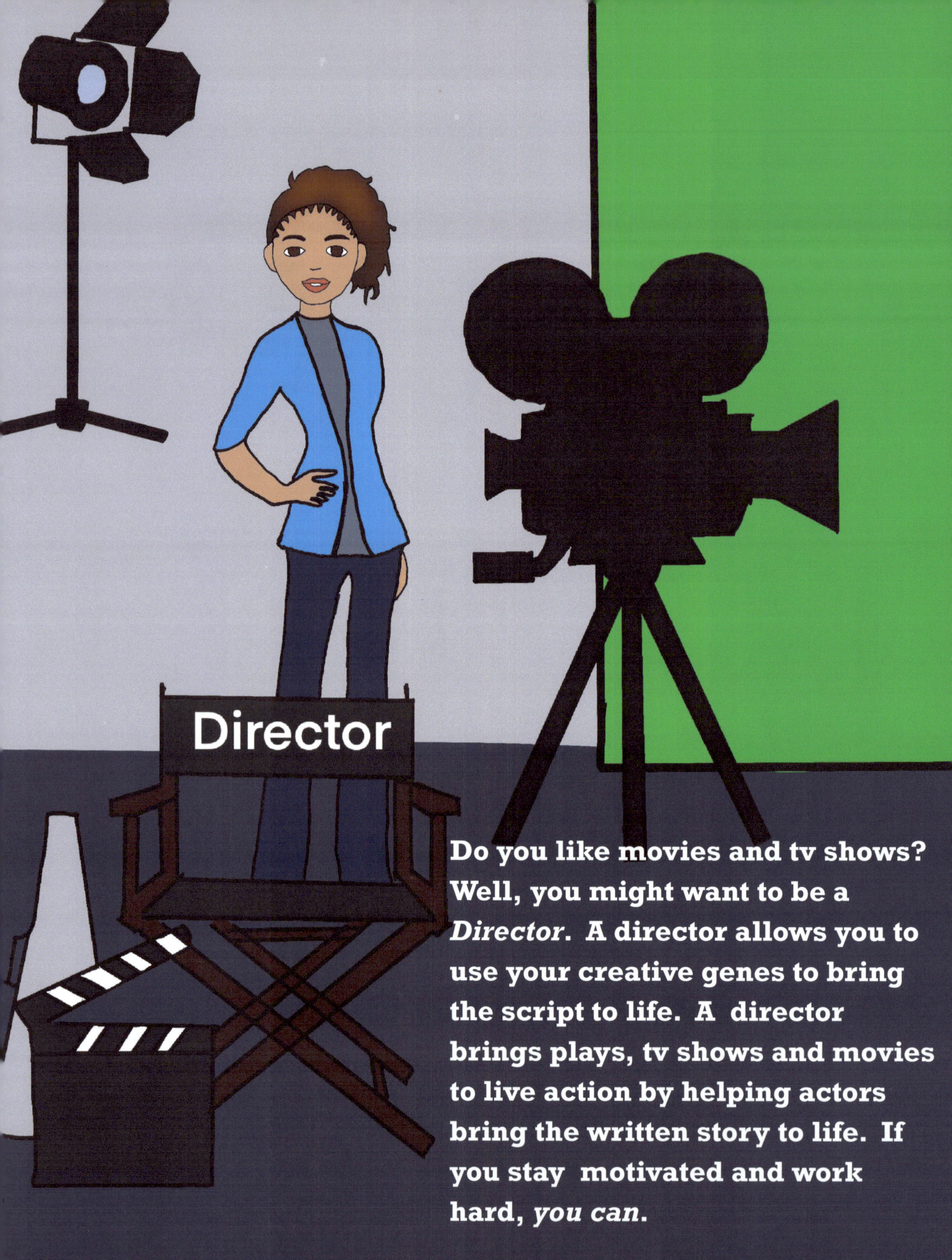

Director
Do you like movies and tv shows? Well, you might want to be a *Director*. A director allows you to use your creative genes to bring the script to life. A director brings plays, tv shows and movies to live action by helping actors bring the written story to life. If you stay motivated and work hard, *you can*.

If you like to talk and share your opinion, you might want to be a *Radio Personality* or *TV broadcaster*. These jobs inform and entertain people. With persistence and determination, *you can*.

You Can Young Queen

What about an *Architect*? This job uses creativity and drawing skills. An Architect draws and designs buildings for companies to work in and homes for people to live in. Well, if you stay dedicated and work hard, *you can*.

You can be an *Engineer* if you choose. An Engineer uses inventiveness to help create new ways of doing things. They also help make changes to things to make them better such as machines, electronics and even roads. With persistence and determination, *you can*.

You Can Young Queen

You can be a *Chef* if you choose. This job is where you get to use your creativity to cook incredible food items for people to enjoy. Well, if you stay motivated and work hard, *you can*.

What about a *Realtor*? This job helps people find houses to live in or buildings for companies to work in. With persistence and hard work, *you can.*

You Can Young Queen

If you are interested in beauty trends and hairstyles then you might want to be a *Cosmetologist*. A cosmetologist is a person who does hair, nails and other things to maintain and enhance a person's natural beauty. With persistence and determination, *you can*.

If you like to write and tell stories then you might want to be an *Author*. An author uses their creativity and writing skills to tell stories that convey messages for others to read about. Well, if you stay motivated and work hard, *you can*.

If you are innovative, like fashion and like to draw you might want to be a *Fashion Designer*. This job creates clothing that is sold to the community. With persistence and hard work, *you can*.

If you like helping the community, talking in front of people and persuading people you might want to be a *Congress Woman*. This job helps to make policies and laws to help better a community. Well, if you stay motivated and work hard, *you can.*

You can even be the *President of the United States*, if you choose. If you care about the needs of the people and want to help bring in laws and policies to benefit people you might want to aspire to be the President of the United States. Well, if you stay motivated and work hard, *you can.*

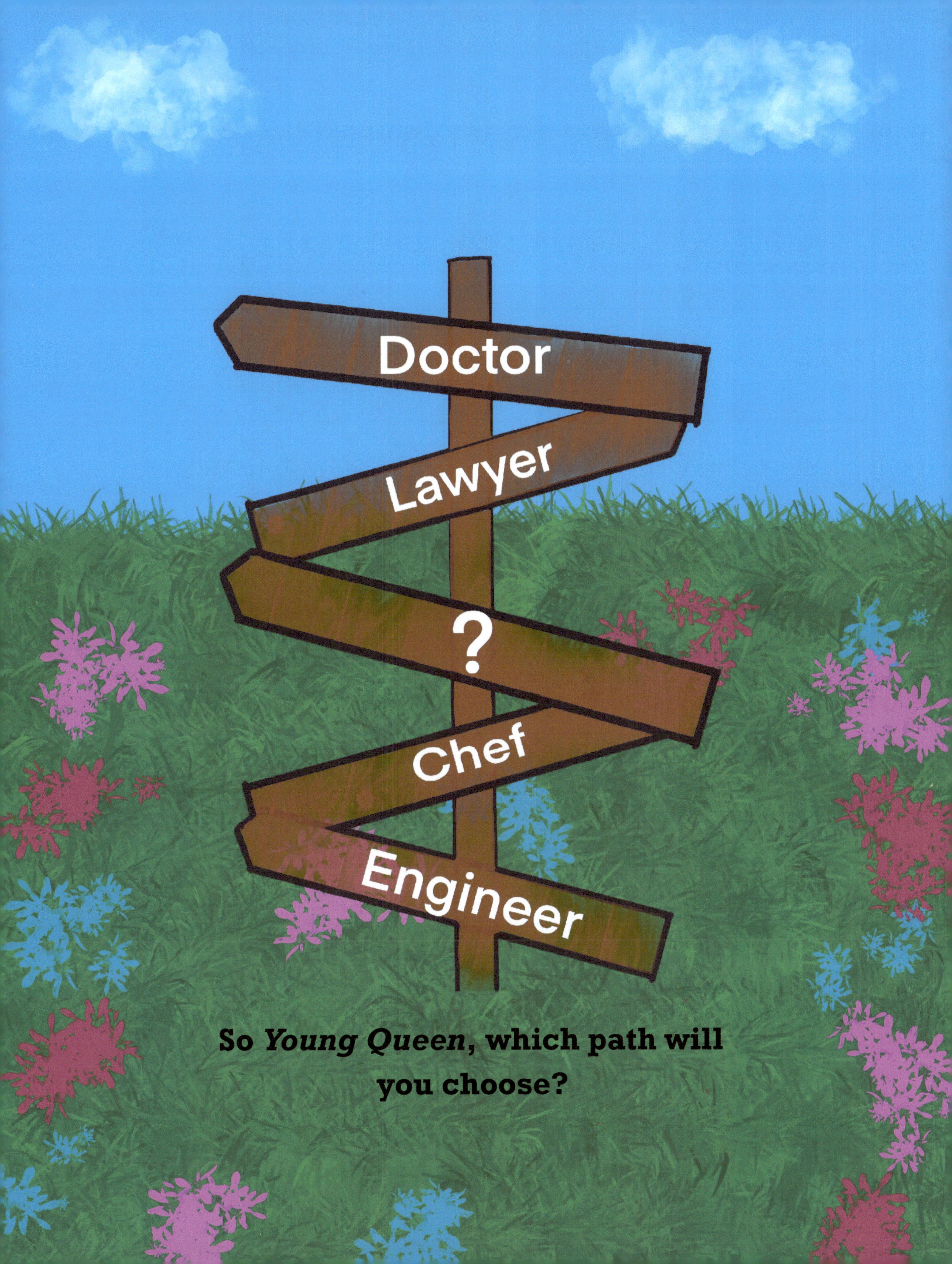

So *Young Queen*, which path will you choose?

What are my interest?

What I want to be when I grow up?

Goals

____

____

____

____

____

____

Steps to Attain My Goals

____

____

____

____

____

____

Goals

Steps to Attain My Goals

Acknowledgments

I would like to thank God with whom all things are possible. My mother (Dorothy) who has always loved, supported, and pushed me to always strive for greatness. My late father (Michael) who instilled in me at a young age to always work hard for my dreams and never give up. My brothers (Michael and Marcus) who have always been there for me and who has shown that hard work and dedication pays off. I would also like to thank my family and friends who have supported me through my journey.

Special thanks to Dorothy, Michael, Marcus, Dominque, Craig, Lindell, Jennifer, Janice, Dorothy T., Mary, Kimberly

www.ingramcontent.com/pod-product-compliance
Lightning Source LLC
Chambersburg PA
CBHW041631110726
48005CB00002B/563